POEMS FOR THE MOTHERLAND

Written by
Josephine Coker

As a tribute to her country

Dedicated to
The Memory of
"Papa-Daddy"
(with Mama MisMay and Mama Adel)
My "Team Ride or Die!"

Poems For The Motherland

Copyright © 2019 by Josephine Coker
All rights reserved

No part of this book may be reproduced in any form or by any electronic or mechanical means except by reviewers for the public press, without written permission from the author.

ISBN: 978-1-9997878-7-5

SONDIATA GLOBAL MEDIA
OWNING THE NARRATIVE

FOREWORD
By Dr Kayode A Robin-Coker

"Poems for the Motherland" is a creative act of sharing and giving back by a poet who evidently values and appreciates what she received by way of a cultural education in the course of growing up in Sierra Leone in the 70s and 80s. Josephine Coker identifies her target audience as "the younger generation now living there", which seems to me an excessively modest aspiration, as I have no doubt at all that a younger generation living not just "there" but ANYWHERE will find this an inspiring, enjoyable, educative and fascinating read. Not only that, but as someone who long since vacated that lobby inhabited by "the young generation" I nevertheless felt, as I read the poems in this collection, affinities with that referenced constituency that can only be the result of the poetry having a greater universality and appeal than perhaps the author herself acknowledges or realises. This is not itself an unusual happening with poetry; it speaks to that quality to which my favourite poet William Wordsworth alludes in the phrase – "we feel that we are greater than we know".

This is neither an incidental nor an accidental publication; each poem sparkles with talent aforethought. An academically gifted alumna of the Methodist Girls High School (one of the oldest and most respected secondary schools in Sierra Leone where, as she recalls in a recent conversation, she was taught how to "understand, interpret and appreciate poetry"), Coker, perhaps not surprisingly, writes poetry that is metrically felicitous, with stylishly rhythmic effects and characterised by skilful, formal and competent use of rhyme. Assured expression and impressive precision come as second nature to a writer with an LLB degree in her toolkit, a writer whose "day job" has encompassed successful careers and formal academic qualifications in the demanding fields of insurance and marketing. Some of these poems read like the sort of accomplished broadside ballads that were popular in the 19th century English poetic tradition.

This collection has an overtly didactic purpose – Josephine Coker started her working life as a qualified teacher in Sierra Leone and it should therefore come as no surprise that "Poems for the Motherland" does not just look back with nostalgia; it also looks forward by aspiring to teach and inspire cultural and academic learning in students in mid-secondary school.

The signature Poem "Mons Panthero" is a heartfelt ode to Sierra Leone. Intriguingly, there is a hint of brooding darkness in the tone of this poem which speaks to the complexity of memory that is at times celebratory but just as frequently regretful of what inevitably came to pass. A lament for bygone days certainly suggests itself in these lines:
Your children cry …
I hear the distant wails,

Of the freed. Their souls cry from the deep.
From chains and shackles we sailed
To adorn thee O Mons Panthero,
And thy brim we did crown;
O Mons Panthero, what ailest thou?

But our poet clearly has a sustaining belief in the restorative powers of Nature (the overarching title of this opening section), and so there is, ultimately, a positive resolution, evident in the defiant, upbeat response by the mountain itself:
I am bled but still not dry.
I am Mons Panthero – I am enough! I am Mama!
Yet, the hills and the valleys
Re-echo the cries,
While the issues, well, they bleed cry.
We love you Mons Panthero
As you weep for us,
May blessing and peace be thine.
Mons Panthero!

She goes on to celebrate the entire country by writing about specific landmarks in Freetown where she grew up, in poems such as "St John's Maroon", "Beyond Freetown" and perhaps inevitably, the iconic "Cotton Tree", which is invested with prescient qualities:
She stands stout
She stands tall,
She has clout
She does not fall...

Her roots span her reign
Come sunshine come rain;
You can see 'tis plain
The Cotton Tree subdues her terrain.

Also featured are her experiences of going to the provinces, particularly the city of Bo where she spent many school holidays while her parents worked there. As a true product of the city of Freetown's Central 2 ward, she captures some of her experiences growing up in that locality in the poems "Saturdays", "Samba Gutter", "Games We Played" and "Dong Tong" (Down Town).

In "Sani Abacha" our poet gives a nod to contemporary issues by referencing the renaming of Kissy Road, Freetown in apparent gratitude to the Nigerian military leader who provided military support for the Sierra Leone government during the civil war. And, she asks:
Why not?
Gratitude is a virtue.
He came and helped in the time of need,
When with heart, soul and dermis,
we did bleed;
We could hardly feed
Our call he did heed.

She however calls for an equivalent, if not similar recognition of national heroes of the same war
What about

the sons of the soil?
Well 'tis their call you may proffer
They must be loyal to the Mother.
But if gratitude is a virtue
And attitude is our fortitude,
Name a lane or vale
To remember,
that just after December
There was bloodshed and embers;
We await, yes we await ...

Reflecting another fallout from the civil war – the over population of the capital city leading to deforestation and floods – is the poem "Waterfalls in the City" while "The Zebra" is an infomercial to educate about the purpose and use of Zebra Crossings. Ms Coker's inspiration for this humorous take on road safety was a conversation with a *keke* driver during one of her recent visits to Freetown. The driver argued that he did not need to stop at zebra crossings as people were meant to run across them. His clincher was that "even the name zebra should tell you that, as it is a fast animal":

He lies on the road
As dead as the proverbial dodo,
But yet he is as alive as he is dead.
For he is a signal
To all who will hearken,
By sight or by listening
That to avoid being dead,
Over him you make your crossing.

Poems such as "The Life of Konkobo" and "The Episode" should set younger readers on a journey of discovery. I was somewhat wrongfooted by "The Palm Tree"; as that happens to be the symbol of the ruling political party in Sierra Leone I thought the poem would have a political message but in fact, like "Mangoes" and "Dapper Fishes of Sierra Leone" it celebrates the richness of some of the offerings of Sierra Leone's fertile soil:

You are so blessed,
Though at times you look stressed,
You do not fall over,
Though you bend like a quiver.

All your parts serve your masters,
Even left overs,
Are used with much candour.

Our poet also celebrates Sierra Leonean music and cuisine (which she appears very partial to) in the thematic grouping of "Rainbow of Music", "Jakitomboi & Jolabete", "Foofoo Soup" and "Beans Akara".

In "Salone Korpoh" she explores the decline of the local currency while more overtly contemporary issues like love and infidelity – an increasingly widespread cultural anomaly – feature in "Shaka's Territory" and "Evening Stroll", the latter something of a cautionary tale for men with wandering feet, as the story of Papa's untimely end is recounted:

At an ungodly hour, she hears a thud,

Who's there at such a time?, the thought!
And like a well-timed execution,
The disappearing act reverses without a pulse.
Check his chest there is no hearbeat.
"Pipul Pikin" is dropped, arriving by night mail,
Mail boat was late so there's no hand over.
Papa don die, who can they ask?
He did not say where he was going,
Lajilah aye, dis na big berrin.

"Welcome" is inspired by recollections of *Komojade* ceremonies in Sierra Leone, where part of the celebrations would include taking the newborn outdoors to 'show them the way'. Coker does her own virtual *komojade* in this poem.

The closing poem in the collection, "The Potion", is a patriotic call to learn from history, set our differences aside, unite and work for the common good going forward. There is a useful glossary of unusual words and phrases which should further enhance the accessibility of the allusive references in the text.

The author's accurately perceived and stated consciousness of a "cultural discontinuity" (or, as she puts it as well, a "culturally deficient inheritance") in Sierra Leone is clearly the creative driver and core motivation for this collection of poems, As she rightly observes, a series of "tragic disruptions" such as the 11 year Civil War, the Ebola and other health epidemics such as cholera, mudslides, etc have resulted in an alienated generation for whom "normality" has gone hand-in-hand with a rather tenuous grasp of historical and socio-cultural realities.

Can poetry heal such fractures, bridge such chasms or reverse such setbacks? On the evidence of this collection the answer has to be a resounding "yes"; while not claiming to have the magic bullet (perhaps, with hindsight, not my best pun) Josephine Coker has certainly been successful in creating a delightful cocktail of judiciously-chosen subjects and images consistent with her artistic aims, which is the hallmark of good and enduring poetry.

Kayode Adesimi Robbin-Coker
Chelmsford, UK (MMXIX)

A WORD FROM THE AUTHOR

The main inspiration for this book is a nostalgic desire to share some of the experiences I acquired growing up in Sierra Leone in the 70s and 80s with the younger generation now living there. It is no secret that a lot has befallen us as a Nation in recent times. First it was the war, then Ebola and other health epidemics such as cholera, mudslides, etc. The war served to accelerate the then budding mass exodus of young people from the country as they sought to escape the worsening economic conditions and seek better lives elsewhere.

These tragic disruptions have been catalysts for the worsening of historically embedded socio-economic problems resulting in cultural discontinuity. Our young people therefore, for the most part, have not benefitted from the incidental learning that comes from daily experiencing the generic cultural legacy from the generation before, thus breeding a glaringly obvious lack of knowledge and understanding of 'normal' life before their time. This void means education is needed as to the whys and hows of contemporary living, particularly in the capital city.

While they must be applauded for their bravery in striving to make do in the toughest of circumstances in which mere survival is no mean achievement, theirs is still a culturally deficient inheritance. Sadly, they, for the most part, do not know what they do not know. I see them therefore as soldiers, born into a 'war' of societal dysfunctions that they did not create. Some of the by-products of this 'war' are evidenced in initiatives such as "Hands Off Our Girls"; even their progenitors would have found some of these trends quite difficult.

This book, while it does not pretend to be the answer to this malaise, is hoped will contribute in its own small way towards bridging this gap in cultural inheritance. The poems are written for the enjoyment of all and sundry as they will no doubt evoke nostalgic memories in the minds of those who lived in Sierra Leone, particularly Freetown, in the 70s and 80s; the era just before the start of the tragic happenings mentioned above. Particularly however, they are written with the younger generation in mind who, in irrigating the imagery used, will hopefully get a better grasp of their cultural inheritance and a better understanding of the way some things are.

In the hope that all my readers will enjoy this work, I have included some poems which reflect transgenerational contemporary living, particularly, in Freetown. For example, poems about staple dishes and love relationships like Shaka's Territory, Foofoo Soup and Jackitomboi and Jolabete will capture the experiences of most people. However, the poem about mangoes I am sure, will educate some about types of mangoes we have in Sierra Leone.

My constant orientation while writing these verses is my memories of exploring poetry in middle and senior secondary school in Freetown. It is my ambition therefore that younger readers of these poems will go on similar journeys of discovery on which they encounter strands of our history as they understand the messages in the verses.

I hope you enjoy reading *Poems For The Motherland*.

Josephine Coker

ACKNOWLEDGEMENTS

First and foremost I want to thank God for the opportunity to put this book together. This exercise, like many such, has not been void of challenges. Nonetheless we pulled through.

I have to thank my Grandfather, the late John Abioseh Wilson, to whom this work is co-dedicated, who though deceased continues to be a major influence in my life. I am what I am today, largely because of this man and I am forever grateful. *Yu tu nor de!*

Thank you Mummy, I am here because of you.

Thank you to my son who constantly interrupts my work just to check that I am ok. I really appreciate that.
To he who knows himself, thank you for allowing me to be me and for encouraging me to do whatever I want to do and be whatever I want to be. "I-AM-A-T" you are special.

I would like to thank the indomitable Khaday Mansaray who has been a constant source of encouragement, inspiration and a battle-axe to get me to deliver despite full knowledge of the many obstacles. We all need friends like her whose sympathy is lined with intolerance for self-pity.

My thanks also go to those who read and reviewed the manuscript. Time is precious, especially in the West. I am grateful for investing a fraction of your life in this work.

Finally, I wish to express my gratitude for the wonderful resource that the internet is as I was readily able to access free stock pictures to help bring the text alive.
It is said that there is a book in every one of us; I have delivered mine!

Josephine Coker

CONTENTS

                                                                  Page No

Nature

Mons Panthero	2
Rivers	4
The Cotton Tree	5
Waterfalls in The City	6
The Palm Tree	8
The Life of 'Konkobo'	10
Mangoes	12

People and Places

St John's Maroon	15
Samba Gutter	16
Outside Freetown	18
Bo City	20
Sani Abacha	22

Food and Culture

Shaka's Territory	24
Games We Played	27
Dong Tong	29
Salone Korpoh	30
The Office Gossip	33
Evening Stroll	36
Rainbow of Music	38
Abu Tailor	40
The Zebra	42

Welcome	44
Saturday	46
Seaweed	49
The Hawker's Cry	51
Jakitomboi & Jolabete	53
Foofoo Soup	55
Beans Akara	57
Dapper Fishes of Sierra Leone	59
The Episode	60
The Potion	61

NATURE

Mons Panthero

Mons Panthero
Thou daughter of Felidae,
What ailest thou?
Thy streams birth life
Thine arbres lush and green
So what ailest thou Mons Panthero?

Are the hills not high enough,
Or the echoes of the vales not clear?
Oh Mons Panthero, what ailest thou?

Your children cry,
Learning is beside thee much
Thou Athens of these shores.
Oh that was a whisper long gone.
I hear the distant wails,
Of the freed. Their souls cry from the deep.
From chains and shackles we sailed
To adorn thee O Mons Panthero,
And thy brim we did crown;
O Mons Panthero, what ailest thou?

Hark! Mons Panthero we hear,
Your deep calls, for you cannot be silent
While your children cry;
Deep calls to deep
The breasts of Mons Panthero drip,
Forever, as she sighs!
Oh the issues of my thighs.
Feed, take your fill.

What ails you Mons Panthero?
Tectonic forces, volcanoes, present at your birth,
Droop and mourn.
Mons Panthero, where we sojourn.
Are you weak, formed by earth, wind, floods or fire?
Alas no!
Diamonds, bauxite, cacao, nuts, oils;
I am bled but still not dry.
I am Mons Panthero – I am enough! I am Mama!
Yet, the hills and the valleys
Re-echo the cries,
While the issues, well, they bleed cry.
We love you Mons Panthero
As you weep for us,
May blessing and peace be thine.
Mons Panthero!

Rivers

The flow, high and low
The Moa, The Sewa
And yes, The Mano calls by too
"Parlent-elles Francais?"
Would the Sherbro flow?
Would our neighbourly 'Mehs', help bestow?

The Great Scarcies, oh you mean Kolente River
Or the Little Scarcies, that is Kaba River
The Rokel skips merrily through mountain terrain
Damn!, the Bankasoka, lest we forget
There is the Jong, and that is how long?
We'll find its claws as it digs deep
Into Atlantic silt

Arise, make haste, the moon's lit
On the crunching sand we can no longer sit
Anon, on the morrow we shall arise to our grit
And dance to the tune of the loom.

The Cotton Tree

She stands stout
She stands tall,
She has clout
She does not fall.
Not for wind or rain,
To char her is vain.
Her roots span her reign
Come sunshine come rain;
You can see 'tis plain
The Cotton Tree subdues her terrain.
Nought will she maim
Dignified as a dame,
What?! She is not lame
Nor can any man tame,
Not with ladder nor with crane
Lest I say with cane,
Yet you cannot say she's vain.
We may not know her pain
Nor can we know her shame,
But she's seen the game
From before they came.
Our stout dame,
Of the realm of the free
The Cotton Tree.

Waterfalls in The City

The once fertile rich and thirsty land
Marched, parched with aplomb!
Through November to March's sun,
And being filled without much till
Going back, October to April

These arcs of time seem to have lost,
Their meeting points on this compost.
As one the other tries to outdo,
With extreme blasts of stripes in each one's hue.
The drier months scorch and parch,
The ground is crinkled, very arid.
In wetter weather as if they seek to kill,
Waterfalls tumble from the hills.

They make their way by force by fire,
With prowess which seems not to tire.
Violating life, transgressing space,
Trespassing blockage, leaving in their wake;
Wanton destruction, pools and lakes.
Every cranny, every nook,
Water around every crook.
Not deterred they power through,
As if to fill the bays and seas.

They do not heed the shrieks and cries,
Seem to do just as they please.
With powering might they just ease,
Through streets and buildings, carrying fridges,
Furnished wood, plastic, ceramics.

They fling wide doors, they break down walls,
None understand these Waterfalls.

The throngs call out loud and long,
Alas they do not rhyme in song,
They panic, fret as they run checks,
While those untouched wonder "what the heck?".
The city's fall came long before,
The rains and mudslides, storms and all.
To rein in check, not ask "what the heck?"
'Tis wise that we remove the speck,
Or ere before it reigned supreme,
Was it a mote, Indeed a beam:
The capital before these streams,
Was swamped by falls of human beings.

They forayed in and made their way,
By ousting mangroves and other trees.
Surrounded by shacked walls of roof tin,
Making nature the enemy therein.
So as seasons change, the arcs swing,
We continue to see the sin;
And feel the wrath of judgement still,
From these ere city waterfalls.

The Palm Tree

You are so blessed,
Though at times you look stressed,
You do not fall over,
Though you bend like a quiver.

All your parts serve your masters,
Even left overs,
Are used with much candour.

Your leaves when stripped,
Give us a broom;
From what is left of it,
We form a loom.

The kernel boiled
Can give palm oil,
Or a delicate snack,
If sweetened with sugar.

The seed is cracked open,
Out pops the nut,
And when that is sodden
Nut oil is got.

Your flesh once sodden
And left in the open,
Can kindle a burning
Fire in the open.

The tapper manoeuvres
Around your trunk's corners,
His bully recovered
Provides man with fresh powers.

Which part of you
From stern to bough;
Does not imbue
Man's lot that he's due?

The Life of 'Konkobo'

The life of Old Riley
Was Pat Rooney's story,
Of 1880.

That was a mirage
Creating a façade,
Like a blockage
To Konkobo's parade;
When in full rage
Or turning the page,
That the real life of folly
Was never told in story.

Ask me not how he got there
The tapper cannot, will not dare,
Ascribe to his glory
This wanton story,
Of our friend Mr *Tumbu*
Don't know if he's from Humbu.

But in the tapper's fare,
He is such a dare!;
You will find him inebriated
You may think that he fainted,
He is clearly painted
In the stripes of the tainted.

Not known to pull a punch
I can tell, and it is a while before lunch,
Our dear friend's on the rungs

And cannot tell that it's dawn,
Because he's filled more than his lungs
With the tapper's fare.

And so he lives
At the end of the *buli*,
Now you've heard the story
And it's not one of glory,
So forbid this to be your tally
Living in folly,
Of this life beware.

Do not fill your trunk
Even if your feelings have sunk,
With Konkobo's tipple
Or you will feel the ripple,
Worse still be called an *obo*
For living the life of the idle
The life of Konkobo!

Mangoes

What luscious leaves
Swaying at ease,
In the gentle breeze
Without a care or a tease.

The trees have come out to play
In the heat of high-day,
And striving hard in their contest
We hear them tell who is the best.

I am *Labayru*, slender and cute
Easy to handle, not obese, obtuse.
That's not quite true
Stop this ruse,
They call me that, but I am not common
Just look at me, evergreen,
Sweet Sixteen.

Please take a bow have you not seen,
My glorious twinings, quite pristine.
T'is a lie in hope,
That I am called *Rope-Rope*.

Please move over
And take cover,
I am a lover not a rover;
There is a reason
I am Lady Damsin.

Oh fair maidens
With all your reasoning,
The best of life's innings
Is always the *Granpikin*.

Now that makes me think
There is a link,
If size were your glory
I am the *Small Cherry*.

You must be leary
To tell a story,
Where the stout hearted merry,
I can't rest easy,
I am the *Big Cherry*!

People and Places

St John's Maroon

We came
From far-flung shores,
From far and wide
Against the tide
We did arrive;
On these banks
And gave our thanks
Against this majestic trunk.

Lest we forget
How we did get
From shackles to tackles;
And now we arrive
After grinding axles,
So we gave thanks
On these banks.

So to keep in our hearts
How we did depart,
We raised an epitaph
To our Rod and our Staff.
In time of grief
In time of need,
Or e'er we rejoiced
At our Ebenezer we plead.

Samba Gutter

Tide without a rudder,
With more than a flutter
It can get out of kilter,
At Samba Gutter.

When the season is dry
It can be a little wry,
But please do not try
For it can be sly.

When tame it looks lame
Staying in its frame,
Like a dame in shame
Good at her game.

But it recovers with usury
When you test its fury,
And then in a hurry
It pays penury.

You cannot be jittery
It can be quite slippery,
While you wash your livery
It can get inflammatory,

Do not be fooled
By the small pools,
If you slide it can pull
And it will have rule.

It survives with largesse
From years of experience,
It outlives many torrents
And some quite great currents.

Many waters it brings
From as wide as it flings,
And pulls downstream
Central's Johnson Spring.

Outside Freetown

Have you gone
Past Mile 91?
The land is a beauty.
The breeze from the hills,
Produces the chills.
We need it ,
We want it ,
In this land of the sun.
To some this is a mystery,
But listen to our story,
Sierra Leone, an ex-colony,
Has more than the palm tree.
Bo gives us gari
Makeni, gara
Masanke, palm oil
Bakasonka, power
Kono has diamonds
Marampa, bauxite.
The land is so glorious,
The people industrious.
From far and wide
We must realise,
Our brethren
They strengthen
This land with their leaven.
There are rice paddies
Groundnut, cassava
Potatoe, piassava
Corn, ore and timber;
And more is left over,

We need to explore
For there is so much more
Than we would ever reckon,
In our Sierra Leone.

Bo City

From Dambara to the clock
I hear ticktock,
There no stop
Sewa Road is round the block.

I climb up the hill
With perseverance,
To crown my deliverance
There is Reservation.

On my return
I am relieved, in joy,
Adjacent to this hill
CKC boards its boys.

I still try to wander
To the paddies out yonder,
Water Street, Bojon Street
Swamps then down town.

As a girl from Freetown
I remember trotting,
As far as I can wander
The streets of Bo exploring.

Buwa I am greeted
Biseh I answer,
But my tongue's limitation
Is soon my explanation.

Yet I was safe
Despite a few scrapes,
As I tried each day
To navigate Mende.

All said and done
I loved the adventures,
And even the creatures
I found in Bo Tong!

Sani Abacha

Why not?
Gratitude is a virtue.
He came and helped in the time of need,
When with heart, soul and dermis,
we did bleed;
We could hardly feed
Our call he did heed.
But then, we must ask
Is it only Uncle Sani
That has heeded our call?
What about
the sons of the soil?
Well 'tis their call you may proffer
They must be loyal to the Mother.
But if gratitude is a virtue
And attitude is our fortitude,
Name a lane or vale
To remember,
that just after December
There was bloodshed and embers;
We await, yes we await ...

FOOD AND CULTURE

'Shaka's Territory'

You said you loved her
And so you woo'ed her,
She struts past, you are aghast.
But for your melanin
You would have been
White as a ghost,
Or as one that has seen
Something shot off-screen.

Little by little
With your tittle-tattle,
As bone that is brittle
You gently break her mettle.
And now on every moonshine
No matter the clime,
Your chest is a mattress
For her head to caress.

This is just as nature ordered
For this prize a man bothers,
By the sweat of his brow
His love to bestow,
And pull along in tow
A fair maid in full glow.

And then the time comes
When with pomp and with song,
You send along your dowry
You have won your prized glory.
And before long

Was that your intention?
Her midriff has become
Your sole invention.

It expands it stretches
The breasts no longer oranges,
But now water melons.
None of the world's breeches,
Can hold back the ravages.
After nine months in time
We hear her wail and whine,
And then through her girth
To your offspring she gives birth.

Son of Shaka Zulu
One will not do you,
Your story we hear
Loud and clear.
Your prize glory shashays
Your eyes open wide,
You make your forays
Into those hidden alleys.

Oh fair lass
Again it comes to pass,
Love's toxicity
Tests your elasticity.
You pop them out
With such clout,
You fill the hood
With your brood.

Now Mr Moonshine remember
That she once was slender,
As your service she's rendered
She must still be your first number.
Do not forget
You passed the test,
You changed her waist and address,
Her mind must now rest.

Games We Played

Clap,
Stamp,
Is that a merry dance
I hear in a trance,
As mama looks askance?
The kids play akra.

Shake,
Waist,
From the land of Bai Bureh
Shake my shegureh,
Beat the "agereh".
Ambo shekusheh!

Pray,
Stay,
Is there a toll to pay?
As while in our play
The boundaries stay.
Ah pass ya? Nor way, nor way.

Chew,
Fruit,
A citrus loot
To fill my boot,
From the 'hood of St Clement's
Oranges and lemons.

Fly,
Try,
Titles can lie
Hopscotch is dry.
Admonish, chide
We play "Ah die".

Meet,
Greet,
There is nothing much.
Before we lose time
Rule the mainline,
One left, one right, Touch.

Dong Tong!

And everybody gonna sing along
As we sail to the new Jamaica,
Rocking the boat
Making sure it does not tip over,
At the port of Victoria.
Tenderly we touch each other
Feeling the loving arms of Laronda.

As the Records Parade
We in our boleros,
Strut to Sombrero
Alongside our heroes,
Purple Haze.

Down Town,
We Count Down.
On the Yellow Submarine,
Where Virgins, Blow Up.

Kay's at Tropicana,
Together with Isabella.
Around BP it's Paramount,
To ring my Yellow Bell
Or at Brookfields Hotel.

Salone Korpoh

I remember when, we could depend
On Grandpa reckoning his stipend,
In cloven tongues to keep the score
And we would have to ask some more;
As by the time that he told what
Was the amount that he had got,
Our minds would juggle and race uneased
As he would announce, "'tis four guineas".

Grandma would then look askance
One could wonder, where's the romance;
"Your Grandpa needs to grow some more
We no longer live in days of yore,
He might be baffled, creating a kerfuffle,
By counting his readies, creating a scruple".
He's got to watch, pay off the bills,
All he's got, is four pounds four shillings.

It's market day and I am away
To the Electric Board our bill to pay.
And then I'll shimmy down to King Jimmy
And there I'll see if I can cop a kinnie,
Or what if there's more, been brought ashore.
But with all this furore, I can assure
I'll pay no more than "foe korpoh"
This dear "boe penny" will bring home Bo Gari,
Oh this life can be heavy, in the Land of the Free.

Gandpa's fix, is "two en six",
He can get sick, from pulling at those sticks.
Hear him cough, but for "tri en troh",
His chest is rough, but still buys "draw-draw".
Old man is still feeling, he can still play "two shillin'",
I am praying, this won't be his killing.
Send him sailing?, no money to bury him,
For ten pong, sen am go dong.

He struts old bones, and all he owns
See Old Jones, pose with "wan Leone".
A teacher's pay, with any luck,
In this our day, is just "three block".
I think this tent, must repent,
What can be lent, on fifty cents?
Even coconut jelly, on my nelly,
Cannot really, fill my belly.

In these days one cannot, just be counting on one's luck,
The simplest 'chop', is now is a few "blocks".
In these times recent, Nothing is pence or cents,
They are bent, they won't relent,
To see that every cent is spent.
Two hundred 'tawzin', Wai!, Grandpa's 'bozin',
Is what we are ridding, on kerosene.

The shops are filled, our eyes are drilled,
We stretch our gills, can't eat our fill.
Our children's food, none in the hood
Our feet are shod, Onward we plod,
Until crook rubber, goes a-bubber

And hunger slumber, makes us sober.
Our needs are plenty, a gazillion
The point of entry, is "wan milyon".

The Office Gossip

You dare not make a mistake
They'll be gunning for your head on a plate, The snake!
The office gossip
Has been in worship,
At the altar of the boss' desk.
In labour there trying to wrest
The prize of being 'alagba's' pet.

Such a cretin, wormy person,
she knows not they're a dime a dozen.
This 'thing'!
She's not like others,
Being 'lie-lay-lay', her bother.
A sneeze, sails with the breeze.
Lest I say, a cough, a wheeze,
Darling is 'finiwusi' with ease.

She calls you 'Darling',
But then you know she's lying.
'Tis her calling!
Don't be a muppet,
When she needs a puppet;
You see I wouldn't care,
If all she did was shut up and stare.
But this 'ojukokoro' I cannot bear.

Sally lie-londo, has to be wrong,
Yet she has to sound her gong.
Her tongue!
Cannot resist her self- interest,

'Darling my dearest', She says with zest.
Sees your soul ripe for trespassing,
'Come here me loving', As you are passing.
Counts 'alaki' as a blessing.

The thing with this sieve,
Is clear I believe.
She sees!
That those who ply this trade,
Learnt from those with the best grades.
Every morn she opens her tomb,
'Good morning me luv', the imbecile booms.
The 'okuru' of her integrity blooms.

You see, if only she had,
And this is so sad.
Too bad!
The nerve and grit to dare,
To lay her thoughts bare.
To ask the very questions,
She answers with assumptions.
But I'd send her 'alangata', the demon.

The slimy twat,
A real bat.
Upstart!
From behind ivory fence posts
Fires her first shot, the snot.
"Luvly weekend? I like your hair."
Dandogo! nor lego or you'll enter her lair

Although there is no pleasing,
In her leasing there is a lesson.
Unleashing!
That the rule we must learn,
Is that wherever we earn.
She's in every corner on earth,
Not just in our land of birth.
The rule of "Wan Man Geng"'s our girth.

Evening Stroll

Papa's feet are a problem.
They seem to have a will and a way,
As day courts night and work is done,
Candles are lit and children read.
Mama broaches their thoughts serving pap,
Hoping for a completely registered night.
Like a twin-interruption as the children read,
An expired rumination he spits out loud,
"Er erm I need to stretch these legs".
Where are you going and when will you be back?,
"Woman keep quiet I am not moving out".
"This can't be right you've just come in."
"You have not been hired to keep score;
No to yu bon mi?, set yu mot"

Without much care for how she feels,
Old Bones is gone like a whiff of smoke.
You would have thought someone called.
Poor Morkeh what on earth can she do?
The children watch, she had to smile,
Seeks consolation in the fleeting thought,
"The man is right, her brood is safe,
From any harm that may befall,
Big man bikful, pipul pikin".

Sharp ten the eyes of the house she closes,
"Children to bed you have school in the morning."
She leaves the back door half off-latch,
And goes to bed sleeps soundly, no hindrance.
At an ungodly hour, she hears a thud,

Who's there at such a time?, the thought!
And like a well-timed execution,
The disappearing act reverses without a pulse.
Check his chest there is no hearbeat.
"Pipul Pikin" is dropped, arriving by night mail,
Mail boat was late so there's no hand over.
Papa don die, who can they ask?
He did not say where he was going,
Lajilah aye, dis na big berrin.

Rainbow of Music

The bow in the cloud
Is a gift of hope to our crowd.
It foretells,
There is yet hope,
Before man elopes.

Yet there is a message more sublime,
That in this time,
Many hues and rays,
Are displayed ,
In all our ways,
Throughout our days.

So as we beat the drums,
And sound the horns,
As trumpets blow,
And dances flow.

We step aside,
And realise,
That each bow plays a tune,
Be it at noon or at full moon.
The sounds melodious,
Are quite a-plenteous,
Each to his own liking,
Chooses to which tune he shall set a-jiving.

Be it bubu or gumbe,
Foxtrot or Maringe,
Twist or Waltz,
Skyank, double bump or reggae,
From the heart bodies pursue,
The soul's musical hue.

Abu Tailor

I have a dream
And it does stream,
From the great books I've seen.
From ships that came powered with steam.
And From their team.

They came ashore,
From lands of yore,
To see what we saw.

We thumped the pages,
We were of all ages,
And thought we were sages.

That floaty blouse,
Will make me look like a cloud,
My desire is aroused,
I will feel quite proud,
Oh still I browse.

The denim, the skirts; oh the dress!
With that I'll surely impress.
I dream of the sweet caress,
Of that garb pressed
Against my chest,
Or on my backrest.

I see me,
Feeling free,
Like a tree,

In the wind.
And I sing,
As I spring.

What will I not give,
To wear that sleeve?
Though 'tis a world of make believe.
It's time will pass just like a breeze,
But for now, it will do as I please.
So please put my mind at ease,
And once again I'll freely breathe,
Once I float in that sleeve;

Oh Abu Tailor,
Please be my saviour!

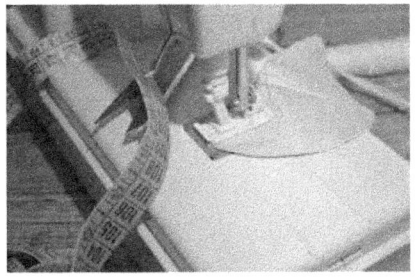

The Zebra

He lies on the road
As dead as the proverbial dodo,
But yet he is as alive as he is dead.
For he is a signal
To all who will hearken,
By sight or by listening
That to avoid being dead,
Over him you make your crossing.

For we have seen many who sped
Without an eye batting,
If you know what you are doing
And really should be driving,
You must pay obeisance
To the allegiance,
Of the code of the road.

For at the Zebra Crossing
You must be a-stopping,
No engines revving.
While you await those a-crossing.
Those stripes on the road,
Are not there for show
Taxi, keke, go slow,
You must pipe down low.

'Tis not to your delight
But it is your brother's right,
Not to take flight
At this beast's demise.

He lies dead to give life
So whate'er the strife,
Stop or you will pay the price
Now or ere life is no more rife
If you maim or take a life.

Welcome

We welcome you
O child of the sun,
To the continent of melanin
Where in life you can win.
Listen to those who have come before
And follow what they have to say,
The sun can be hot
But if you listen up,
You would have come to play.

There is Mama, there is Papa
Where the sun burns,
There is always Grandma and Grandpa,
Aunties are plenty,
Uncles are a bounty,
And all your neighbours will be cousins.
There is no choosing,
There is no fussing,
They are there just because
The sun on its course,
Brought them in.

This is true
For all Africa's daughters and sons.
At the breaking of the morn,
Once you are born.
You are a part of the clan,
From places far and wide.
But listen up, listen up,
There are rules to this tan.

Mama and Papa, their words are scripture,
Grandma and Grandpa, their counsel nature.
For the heads of the aged,
Spew the vitriol of sages.
As you turn through life's pages,
You will sure reap the wages.

Aunties and Uncles,
They are life's carbuncles.
Neighbours, nay cousins,
They can be lesions.
It's up to you, what's your vision.

Within the clan,
See how far it spans?
You have your teachers,
Yes they can be leechers;
But return the favour
And settle the score,
Or you'll be none the wiser
Force open the door,
And be a breacher.

There is sun,
There is fun,
In the hood,
The food is good.
Join in,
Play the game,
As we look on
The world is your frame.

Saturday

Uniforms to wash
That includes socks,
All our vestments
And our bed's garments,
Are soaked in Surf
In a mighty froth.

Hide and tripe
Cockle and pig's knuckle,
All are boiled
The harvest of toil,
Topped with palm oil
Which creates a soil.

Foofoo on a plate
From Bullom's shore,
Mixed leaves to placate
Ogirie, ogusi, condiments galore.
What can I smell?,
Give me some more.

The whole house is stripped
And brought to its knees,
Only to be rebuilt
Shining like a new pin.
Floors swept and polished,
Chairs and tables varnished.
Rugs shaken and beaten,
Curtains changed or are shaken.

Dust is lost,
Clean walls are a must.
Fresh spreads on the beds
Holes mended with threads,
Shoes wiped down and polished
Ridden of all rubbish,
Picked up as we fared
Through the week's year.

Clothes on lines jubilating
Can almost hear the singing,
As they dance to the echo
Of the wind as it blows;
Wafts of Destree and starch
Are caught in the garments' arch,
As if to say hello
Ekusheh, Great doing.

The whole yard is swept
All small rooms are kept,
You'll pardon your nostrils
As with fresh scent,
They flare in the breeze.
Pressers are lit
They join the retreat,
Of the end of the week
They ensure we are neat.

When the singing is done
The wind ends its song,
The sun takes a bow

Garments are withdrawn,
Folded to show
The labour bestowed.

Everything's put away
Chickens stop their play,
Sunday stew is done
Tomorrow is for fun;
And those in their prime
Come out pristine,
In the shadows, sublime
After they have dined,
They are on-line
For earned downtime.

Now our labour's done
Tomorrow to worship and rest,
We will don our best
And feather our nests.
The year of next week
Will soon on us creep,
The hussle continues
Aluta! Well done!

Seaweed

As I navigate these straits
Hindered by these entangled strands,
I try to make my way through
Not a brush nor a comb would do.
On this crown, with a frown
I struggle to get through.

Ouch, it pains, as I pull on my veins,
I need a moisturising solution
Or an even stronger potion,
To help me manoeuvre
And reach the shore of my grandiose.
Onward I press
Until I can bounce my tress.

Wai, hmmm, eeeeshhh, woi, ouch,
I'm still on this couch,
Pulling, stretching, tugging
My head is now buzzing.
What more can I say?
But I still need to stay,
On this course to my haven
To display the prize woven.

And so onward I press
As I tug and caress,
I part and divide
And with a slide I hold a line,
Until the whole crown shines,
And the dividing lines

Set a course for the breaking,
Of fashion's fair haven.

Phew! Alas!, It has come to pass,
I can now pull through
Without a huff or a puff,
My comb's a fair compass
To navigate this atlas.
There is no more road block
As I stretch my kinky locks.

Like a true sun-bleached maiden
I never give up, Until I reach my stop.
I reach my haven,
I deftly create, lovely bouncy braids.
See my tresses droop
I can even make a loop,
Oh yes, another scoop
These braids can form a hoop.

These knotted weeds, sea weeds
of a Nubian lass,
Can be quite resistant
To my fair compass.
But with bent
insistence
And inbred resilience,
I arrive at the shore
Of beauty displayed,
galore.

The Hawker's Cry

My ears are pricked
I hear wails, cries, screams,
"ah get di bologi",
"fayn pamine ya".
"ah get di fayn tamatis",
"Langa mina yaaaaa".

What's that I'm asked,
Why does she weep?
Is trouble afoot;
Or is that a soul uncouth?

No dearest friend.
From days of yore
On these shores ,
The hawkers trade
Is not to set a score,
Or e'er would you have been
At death's door.

The shrill morning cries;;
"Awefu ya".
Is all intact?
For dawn's just cracked.
Be still fair one,
That voice wrests
To claim the rest,
Of gaining the day's best.

Let her cry, let her wail,
Let the sounds sail.
Still the waves of your mind
And remember, remember,
Her toil is to avail
That prize, the prize behind your veil.

Jakitomboi and Jolabete

Jakitomboi, Jolabete.
From the ground
We draw,
iron, zinc, magnesium.
Oh we are so blessed,
Just put it to the test,
Excuse me while I lick my spoon.

Aha, as I was saying,
While you were looking,
At me licking
My palm-oil dressed lips;
No I did not kiss,
To enjoy this bliss.
Aha, excuse me while I lick my spoon.

Like I just said,
I have not bled.
The red you see,
Comes from the kernel tree,
And makes me see,
What you show to me.
But wait, excuse me I have to lick my spoon.

Aha, like I was saying,
While you were laying
An open watch in awe,
As I guzzled some more,

Of this divine preparation
Leading to my elation.
But yes, I need to lick my spoon.

Since you've tarried long,
As I sing this song,
Accept my invitation,
To enjoy tjchis elation.
Come taste of this concoction,
And help me make the proclamation.
Aha – I need to lick my spoon.

Yes, like I told you,
See, now you enjoy it too.
No wait you cannot go it alone,
While I suck on my bone,
I need to wipe that plate,
Sorry you are too late.
Oh yes, and now I lick my spoon;
Ha you sound like it's full moon.

Foofoo Soup

One, Two, Three,
Stop counting
I have far to go yet,
No matter how much I sweat
But that belly is under threat,
I hear the moans of that vest.
Yes I need to put to the test,
The cavities of my chest.

Four, Five, Six,
What is this?
Can't I have some peace?
Life can't be better than this.
But I hear the hissing licks,
As you pull on your digits.
Don't you know this is bliss,
Or have you not heard the term "soup sweet"?

Seven, Eight, Nine,
This is quite sublime.
I hear the clocks, they chime,
But who asked them to keep time,
Or did they spend a dime?;
So tell them I shall ragtime,
When I finish with this dine,
And I will be just fine.

Ten, Eleven, Twelve,
Into nature's yarn let us delve.
It provides for all who abide,

With favour and chide.
The taste you see,
hinged on your spree could be;
Shokotoh Yokotoh, Arata Yace,
Ajefawoe – Eat broke plate;
Shakpa, Bittas, Sawa, Okroh,
Kren-Kren, Green and more galore.

Beans Akara

Wonderful mixture,
Savour the flavour,
Feel the texture,
Hmmm, What a fixture!

The oil is hot,
In the pot,
This is its lot,
So it does not rot.

We have peeled,
Removed the black seals,
And it feels,
Not like an eel.

They are ground,
Hear the sound,
They go around,
Then form a mound.

Check the element,
Forming sediment?,
And the condiments,
For its complement.

Pass the ladle,
'Twill be the paddle.
Ride the saddle,
If you are able.

In they go,
The mixture flows,
Like ducks in a row,
Lined up in tow.

The edges crown,
With golden brown,
They cannot burn,
We flip them around.

And when it's over,
They cannot take cover,
From mouths waiting to devour,
With all power.

Though hot we chop,
Grind and slurp,
Bliss, why not?!
And then we burp.

This goes on till,
We've had our fill,
Set for the kill,
Oh what a thrill.

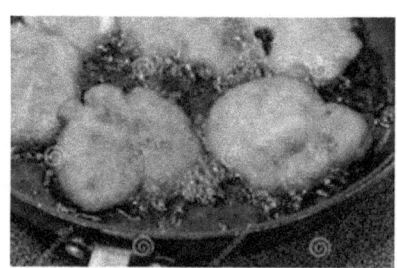

Dapper Fishes of Sierra Leone

Hold me close
My dear Shine Nose,
We are on to a winner
With my Mina.
Play the conga
And wonder,
For I love my Bonga.
I sure will look dapper,
Hooked up to my Snapper.
What a way to be a looker,
With my Kuta.
And can make this life sweeter,
With my Bonita.
Once I've donned my pini,
I'll be with my Kinnie;
And to hear the evening story,
I'll have my Tennie.
Tomorrow I'll be a trouper,
With my Grouper.
Then with this herring,
I'll find my bearing.
And at last have my biscuit,
With my Skit from 'Rikit'.

The Episode

Tom Kyat the Santibokiat,
With upper left, hooks Sorie Tunku,
Stupefied like Book Mumu,
Without a clue, "E damu".

Sorie Arata fleeing Oga,
Cannot pass up on "Penny Kanya".
Throws Dorti Dinah a life line,
Scurries back from Mammi-In-Time,
Who "cooked soup, nor put wata",
With Aunty Sally's Shenge bonga.
Papa Police arrives quick march,
Khaki bristling amply starched.

Sisi Marie, still in her prime,
Flows as she rocks the floor to time,
Like ORS Tunku's alert,
Dis mona,
Papa Police dispatch.

The Potion

What's the reason,
For the tension?
Is there a lesion,
Or an abrasion?
We need fusion
For our expansion.
Love, the ablation
No need for catheterisation.
For wealth creation,
We need interrogation,
An education,
For our redemption.
One people with passion
And sensitisation.
Not Red, Green, just one nation,
We are all relations,
Drinking the potion
Of division;
Basking in the lotion
Of our situation,
With compassion
As our medication,
For our elevation
Good for rumination,
Elucidation,
with inspiration.
So for promotion
And rejuvenation,
Join this marathon
To our destination

Of hate's elimination
And peaceful vibrations
And endless celebration.

A GLOSSARY
Of 'Unusual' Words and Expressions

Abu – an indigenous man's name
Agereh – A drum usually covered with animal skin
Ah Die – hopscotch
Ah get di fayn tamatis – I have nice tomatoes to sell
"Ah pass ya?" – May I pass here?
Ajefawoe/Eat broke plate – a type of leafy vegetable
Akra – A type of children's game where they clap and skip
Alagba – a big powerful person, usually male
Alaki – good for nothing
Alangata – to toss over a distance
Aluta – From the rallying expression 'Aluta Continua', Portuguese for 'The Struggle Continues'
Ambo shekusheh - a musical game
Arata Yace– a type of leafy vegetable
Aunty Sally – a character in a popular local song who went to buy Bonga (fish) and gave birth to a "crying diamond"
Awefu – a type of fish
Bai Bureh – a renowned Sierra Leonean warrior who fought against the British imposition of a Hut Tax in Sierra Leone
Bakasonka – a town in Sierra Leone
Bubu – A type of heavy base musical beat
Beans Akara – Fried balls made from black eyed beans
Big Cherry – A type of mango. Usually large in comparison to others and quite colourful
Big man bikful – an old man who does not act his age
Bikful – big fool

Biseh – Response to greeting in Mende, a Sierra Leonean language from the South
Bittas (a type of leafy vegetable) – A type of leafy vegetable
Boe penny – an old coin with a hole in the middle
Bologi – a type of leafy vegetable
Bonga – a type of fish
Bonita – a type of fish
Book Mumu – a dunce
Bozin – scrotal hernia
Buli – Gourd for collecting and storing palm wine
Buwa – A greeting in Mende, a Sierra Leonean language from the South
CKC – Acronym for Christ The King College, a prominent boys, school in Bo
Conga – A type of musical instrument
Dandogo – a dunce
Dis mona,- lit, This is difficult
Dong Tong – An area of Central Freetown where there was a group of clubs for young people in the 70s and 80s
Dorti Dinah – usually a lady not best known for keeping herself clean
Draw draw – 'sticks' for smoking, in this case cigarettes.
E damu – S/he is gobsmacked
Ekushe – Well Done
Felidae – A big cat
Fayn pamine ya – Fine palmoil available here
Finiwusi - Duplicitous
Flows as she rocks the floor to time
Foe Korpoh – a value of money, around 2 cents
Foofoo – An African starchy food usually eaten with a sauce
Foxtrot or Maringe

Gara – Tie and dye material
Gari – Cassava granules
Granpikin – lit Grandchild; also a type of small and sweet mango found in Greater Freetown
Green– a type of leafy vegetable
Grouper – a type of fish
Gumbe – A type of music indigenous to the Creoles of Sierra Leone with Jamaican Maroon roots
Herring – a type of fish
Jakitomboi - Cooked cassava leaves
Jolabete – Cooked potatoe leaves
Keke – a small motorised vehicle
Kini/Kinnie – a type of fish
Komojade – African naming and outdooring ceremony of a newborn
Konkobo – a type of maggot, reportedly found at the bottom of palmwine gourds
Kono – a major city in Sierra Leone
Korpoh – Money, usually cash
Kren-Kren - a type of leafy vegetable
kuk soup, nor put wata – cook some soup without adding water (lit.) an expression with sexual connotation
Kuta (Barracuda) – a type of fish
Labayru – A slender, usually green type of mango
Langa mina yaaaaa – Long minnows (a type of fish) available here
Lajilah – an expression of surprise
Lego – "let go"
Lie-lay-lay - a compulsive liar
Lie-londo – See 'lie-lay-lay' above
Makeni – a city in Sierra Leone

Mammi-In-Time – used to be a well-known seller of cooked food whose meals were always ready on time
Marampa – a prominent mining city in Sierra Leone
Maringa – a corruption of the Dominican Merengue – a type of music/dance
Masanke – a town in Sierra Leone
Mina (minnow) - sprats
Mons Panthero – Lion Mountains
No to yu bon mi – you did not birth me (lit)
Nor way, nor way - No way, no way
Obo – useless person; sometimes used in a jocular fashion
Oga – the boss
Ojukokoro – envious, coventeous or greedy
Okroh – Okra in English
Okuru - a skin disease usually associated with emaciated dogs
ORS – Oral Rehydration Salts
"Parlent-elles Francais?" – Do they(f) speak French?
Penny Kanya – A penny's worth of a common snack "kanya" usually made from flour, peanut butter and sugar.
Pipul pikin – somebody else's child
Rikit (Ricket) – a fishing village near Freetown
Samba Gutter – A large gutter which runs from the hills to Susan's Bay
Santibokiat – colloquial reference to a thief
Sawa (Sorrel) – a type of leafy vegetable
Sen am go dong – send it down
Set yu mot – literally, 'shut your mouth'
Shakpa - the bulb of the roselle plant (Hibiscus Sabdariffa) used as a vegetable

Shegureh – a hand-held musical instrument made from small gourds, string and beads or cowrie shells
Shenge – a fishing village in Sierra Leone.
Shine Nose – a type of fish
Shokotoh Yokotoh – a type of leafy vegetable
Sisi Marie – the main character from a one-time popular folksong 'Sisi Marie Dans Mi Saful'
Skit – a type of fish
Skyank, double bump or reggae
Small Cherry – A roundish type of mango, usually small and colourful when ripe.
Snapper – a type of fish
Sorie Arata – Sorie the rat (lit.) A thief
Sorie Tunku – a notorious short person
Tawzin – thousand
Tawzin – thousand
Ten pong – ten pounds
Tennie – a type of fish
Three Block – colloquialism for three hundred Leones
Tom Kyat – Tom Cat
Touch – a type of game
Tri en troh – three shillings and three pence
Two en six – Two shillings and six pence
Two shillin' – A colloquial reference to a small brown football which used to be sold for two shillings
Tumbu – lit. maggot
Wai, hmmm, eeeeshhh, woi, ouch- expressions of pain
Wan Leone – One Leone
Wan milyon – One milyon (leones)
Wan Man Geng – literally 'One Man Gang'; a loner

Thank you for reading
       see you in Volume 2 ...

www.ingramcontent.com/pod-product-compliance
Lightning Source LLC
Chambersburg PA
CBHW022341040426
42449CB00023B/1056